The
TREMENDOUS
POWER
OF prayer

A Collection of Quotes and Inspirational Thoughts
to Inspire Your Prayer Life

The TREMENDOUS POWER OF prayer

CHARLIE "TREMENDOUS" JONES
AND BOB KELLY

HOWARD
PUBLISHING CO.

Our purpose at Howard Publishing is to:

- *Increase faith* in the hearts of growing Christians
- *Inspire holiness* in the lives of believers
- *Instill hope* in the hearts of struggling people
  everywhere

Because He's coming again!

The Tremendous Power of Prayer
© 2000 by Bob Kelly and Charlie "Tremendous" Jones
All rights reserved. Printed in the United States of America

Published by Howard Publishing Co., Inc.,
3117 North 7th Street, West Monroe, Louisiana 71291-2227

00 01 02 03 04 05 06 07 08 09   10 9 8 7 6 5 4 3 2 1

Library of Congress Cataloging-in-Publication Data
The tremendous power of prayer : a collection of quotes and
inspirational thoughts to inspire your prayer life / [compiled
by] Charlie "Tremendous" Jones and Bob Kelly.
   p. cm.
  ISBN: 1-58229-131-4
   1. Prayer—Christianity—Quotations, maxims, etc. I.
Jones, Charlie, 1927- II. Kelly, Bob, 1929-

BV210.5 .T74 2000
248.3'2—dc21   00-033604

Edited by Philis Boultinghouse
Interior design by LinDee Loveland

All Scripture references have been taken from the Holy Bible,
New International Version. Copyright © 1973, 1978, 1984
International Bible Society. Used by permission of Zondervan
Bible Publishers.

It's with grateful hearts that we dedicate this volume to our dear friend and brother in Christ, Bob Nease. It was Bob who introduced us to each other many years ago, an introduction that has led to a wonderful friendship. And it was Bob who first suggested that we collaborate on a book, the result of which is the volume you now hold in your hand. Thanks, Bob. You're tremendous!

contents

∞

chapter 1 – prayer is...

15

"Prayer is a summit meeting in the very throne room of the universe. There is no higher level."

RALPH HERRING

∞

chapter 2 – intercession

37

"Intercession is the mother tongue of the whole family of Christ."

DORA GREENWELL

C
ontents

chapter 6 – when to pray

115

"We can come anytime, in any place, with our bodies in any position."

WARREN MYERS

∞

chapter 7 – presenting your requests

131

"The sweetest lesson I have learned in God's school is to let the Lord choose for me."

DWIGHT L. MOODY

∞

chapter 8 – counsel and observations

147

"Let's keep our chins up and our knees down— we're on the victory side!"

ALAN REDPATH

contents

acknowledgments

The quotations and illustrations in this book have been drawn from several hundred volumes in our personal libraries and from other materials we have collected over a period of many years, the sources of which were not always duly recorded. We have made every effort to give proper credit to the original author of each selection, when known. In the event we have failed to acknowledge the correct source of any of this material, we sincerely apologize, and when called to our attention, we will make the appropriate corrections in future editions.

B. K. AND C. J.

introduction

by Charlie "Tremendous" Jones

Have you ever wondered what sort of a guy would have a nickname like "Tremendous"? Well, you're not alone. My friends think it's pretty funny. People who don't know me and come to hear Charlie "Tremendous" Jones speak have no idea what to expect. Some wonder if I'm perhaps the world's biggest egotist. Others figure I'm probably a 350-pound professional wrestler or maybe the spokesman for some sort of new "miracle" cleanser.

Well, the answer is "none of the above." I realize it's a ridiculous nickname, one that's been a source of embarrassment to me for years. For example, whenever I'm staying in a hotel and a long-distance call comes in for me, the operator will usually ask: "Is this Mr. Charles [tee hee] 'Tremendous' [tee hee] Jones?" It certainly isn't a nickname I chose, and I don't wear it because I've accomplished great things. No, the simple truth is that I acquired it solely because of a limited vocabulary!

That's right! Early in my insurance career, whenever one of my agents would report that he or she had sold a policy, I'd respond, "Tremendous!" Or when a young couple at church would announce the birth of their new baby or the purchase of their first home, my reply would invariably be, "Tremendous!" Even the colleague who told me that his mother-in-law had just died was likely to hear "Tremendous." I used the word so often that it stuck, and I've never been able to get away from it or live it down.

No, dear reader, there's nothing tremendous about Charlie Jones. My life story is, in fact, quite simple, a story that takes no more than fifteen seconds to tell. Here it is: *I'm not what I think I am, I'm not what I hoped I'd be, and I'm not what I ought to be. But, by the grace of God, I'm not what I was.* "I once was lost but now am found, was blind but now I see."

There you have it—the story of my life, a testimony to God's amazing grace. His grace, His love, are truly amazing, or, if I may say so, *tremendous!* We do have a tremendous God, who is King of Kings and Lord of Lords.

Just how great, how tremendous is He? Listen to His own words: " 'For my thoughts are not your thoughts, neither are your ways my ways,' declares the LORD. 'As the heavens are higher than the earth, so are my ways higher than your

ways and my thoughts than your thoughts'"
(Isaiah 55:8–9).

How, then, can we possibly interact with a
God whose ways and thoughts are immeasurably
higher than our own? The answer is *prayer!*
Prayer spans the billions of miles between earth
and heaven in an instant; and in that same
instant, we can be ushered into the very throne
room of heaven. We have the incredible privilege of calling on our God—at any hour of the
day or night—confessing our sins, asking His
forgiveness, presenting our petitions, interceding for others, praising Him, and listening for
the sound of His "still, small voice."

Prayer is much more than talking with God.
It's also God's Spirit speaking to us and for us
and moving us to share our thoughts, problems,
and praises with Him. God always hears us as we
pray in Jesus' name: That is His sacred promise
to us, and He is faithful. Saying the "right

words" does not matter to God. He hears our innermost thoughts and desires that can't be expressed in words, and best of all, the Holy Spirit is our interpreter.

In the pages that follow are many quotations on the various aspects of prayer. Some were written by such well-known Christians as O. Hallesby, Oswald Chambers, Charles Spurgeon, Francois Fenelon, and Madame Jeanne Guyon. Over the years, they have blessed my heart richly, and I pray that as you read them, you will discover, as I have, that truly, "Prayer is tremendous."

introduction

by Bob Kelly

Tremendous—what a great word to describe prayer. It's defined, in various dictionaries, in such terms as "extraordinarily great in size, amount or intensity," and as "causing astonishment by its magnitude." Synonyms include *huge, vast, immense, wonderful, amazing, enormous, colossal, marvelous,* and *awe-inspiring*.

Certainly prayer is all of these and more. As the men and women whose words are recorded in the following chapters so eloquently express it, prayer is indeed tremendous. It is

I

tremendous in that it allows us to come before the throne of God; it is tremendous in its power to change lives, in its power to alter the course of history, and in its power to sustain us through the deepest valleys in our lives. Prayer is tremendous as the vehicle that carries our petitions and our praise heavenward.

In my own life, I've experienced the tremendous power of prayer many times. To try to record them all would take more space than there are pages in this book. At the same time, I cannot proclaim that "Prayer is tremendous" without some testimony of God's faithfulness to me. Accordingly, I've chosen the story of what has been, thus far in my life, the most extraordinarily great, immense, colossal, wonderful, awe-inspiring, or simply "tremendous" answer to my prayers.

It was 3 A.M. on June 25, 1977. I was kneeling by my bed in a hotel room in Oradea, Romania, hundreds of miles behind the Iron Curtain. An hour before, I'd been arrested by the Communist police, who had earlier taken my partner into custody for the "crime" of carrying a suitcase filled with Bibles.

We worked for an international ministry dedicated to taking Bibles and other Christian materials into Iron Curtain countries. Sven was an experienced courier, but this was my first trip, and I was terrified. Our van, in which some fifteen hundred New Testaments and songbooks were concealed, had been seized, and I had visions of Communist agents searching it and finding our precious cargo.

We'd been told to report back to police headquarters at 8 A.M. With our secret exposed, I fully expected to be sentenced to a long prison term, as a few other unfortunate Bible "smugglers" had been. As I knelt, close to despair, I thought of my family thousands of

introduction

9

miles away and of the circumstances that had led me, in two short years, from the presidency of a Florida bank to this place, where I had no one to turn to for help.

No one, that is, except God. I opened the small Bible that I always carried to the book of Acts, and I read the story of the miraculous release of Paul and Silas from prison. Trapped hundreds of miles behind the Iron Curtain, our predicament seemed even worse than theirs. Nevertheless, I prayed this seemingly impossible prayer: "Lord, I know You're the same today as You were two thousand years ago, with the same miraculous powers. Open our prison doors, I pray, and restore us to freedom within twenty-four hours."

Later that morning, we endured three hours of questioning, and then, to our amazement, we were told we could leave. Our passports and the keys to our van were returned, and we were on our way. Astonishingly, everything in the van was exactly as we had left it, and the secret compartments were intact.

However, we were by no means out of danger, as three Communist borders and hundreds of miles lay between us and freedom. The Romanian police followed us all the way to the border, where the guards merely waved us through the barriers. The Yugoslav guards did the same as we entered that country. Again, we were closely followed, as day turned into night.

When we got close to the Yugoslav/Austrian border, Sven told me to stop. "We're not allowed to cross at night," he explained, "because traffic is light and the guards pass the time by carefully searching the few vehicles that arrive."

I persuaded him to get close enough for us to check out the situation. To our surprise and delight, the line of cars approaching from the Austrian side seemed endless, and with barely a glance, the busy Yugoslav guards waved us on our way.

As we entered Austria, I looked at my watch. It was 3 A.M., exactly twenty-four hours after I had prayed that seemingly impossible prayer.

Later, the director of our Eastern European operation, a twenty-year veteran of that work, sent a memo to our president, in which he wrote: "The release from a long term in prison for Bob and his partner is one of the greatest miracles we have seen to date in the long history of miracles in connection with this work."

E. M. Bounds once described prayer as "the language of a man burdened with a sense of need. It is the voice of a beggar, conscious of his poverty, asking of another the thing he needs." On that long-ago night, I was such a man. God heard that beggar's voice. Like Jonah, "in my distress I called to the LORD, and he answered me" (Jonah 2:2).

"One of the greatest miracles we have seen...in connection with this work." Indeed, prayer is tremendous!

chapter one
prayer is . . .

"Seek the LORD while he may be found;
call on him while he is near."

ISAIAH 55:6

∞

"I sought the LORD, and he answered
me; he deliverd me from all my fears."

PSALM 34:4

Prayer is a summit meeting in the very throne room of the universe. There is no higher level.

RALPH HERRING

1

prayer is...

A Summit Meeting

Prayer seems to be a very popular topic these days. Articles on prayer and other spiritual subjects have appeared in such major secular publications as Newsweek, Reader's Digest, Time, *and* U.S. News & World Report. *Most of the material in these articles seemed to equate the word* prayer *with petition, asking God for such things as good health or more financial resources.*

Yet praying involves much more than asking God for things we need or want for ourselves, no matter how important or

1

worthy those requests or petitions may be. And prayer is more than reciting words and phrases we've learned by heart. The passage in the New Testament called "The Lord's Prayer" was Christ's direct response to His disciples' plea to "teach us to pray." It is certainly worth repeating, but not if we simply rattle it off by rote, without our hearts and minds in it.

There are many forms of prayer: praising God, interceding for others, confessing our sins, and thanking Him for all the blessings we enjoy. While petition is probably the most common type, prayer has another dimension, which is perhaps the most neglected. Prayer is a "two-way street." Listening to God should always be an important part of our prayer time.

There are those who claim to have literally heard the voice of God, and we would not dispute them. For most of us, however, the voice of God is a "still, small voice" that may come through a passage of Scripture, the admonition of a friend, or an inner conviction that "this is the way; walk ye in it." But if we are to hear that voice, we must quiet our hearts and listen closely; we must, as the Bible tells us, "Be still and know that I am God."

The quotations that follow describe and define prayer in many ways: a golden key, a scourge to Satan, powerful energy, vast and vital, a spiritual gymnasium, fellowship with God, a strong wall and fortress, the breath of the newborn soul, and the nerve that moves the muscle of Omnipotence. May these and the other comments that follow help us get a clearer understanding of how tremendous prayer is, and may we apply it continually in our own lives.

prayer is . . . .

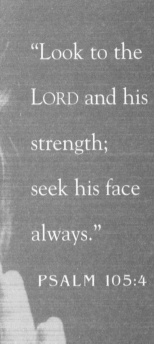

"Look to the
LORD and his
strength;
seek his face
always."

PSALM 105:4

Prayer is not only worship,
it is also an invisible emanation
of man's worshiping spirit—the
most powerful form of energy
that one can generate.

ALEXIS CARREL

"I love the LORD, for he heard
my voice; he heard my cry for
mercy. Because he turned his
ear to me, I will call on him as
long as I live."

PSALM 116:1–2

1 Prayer is vital. It is the pathway to tranquility and peace of soul. A man's prayers are the measure of his Christianity, understanding of spiritual matters, and experience of God. To fail in prayer is to fail in all else. Prayer is the place of testing and conflict; for prayer challenges all doubt, all disillusionment, all material, and cardinal preoccupation.

E. M. BLAIKLOCK

∞

Prayer is not eloquence but earnestness.

HANNAH MORE

∞

Prayer is the voice of faith.

JOHN HOME

Prayer is the slender nerve that moves the muscle of Omnipotence.

EDWIN HARTSILL

∞

Prayer is not a substitute of work, thinking, watching, suffering, or giving; prayer is a support for all other efforts.

GEORGE A. BUTTRICK

∞

Prayer is for the religious life what original research is for science—by it we get direct contact with reality.... We pray because we are made for prayer, and God draws us out by breathing himself in.

P. T. FORSYTH

prayer is . . . .

1

Prayer is a mysterious instrumentality and can, in the final analysis, be employed to full effect and with perfect success only by those who are helpless.

O. HALLESBY

∞

Prayer is not getting things from God, but getting into communion with God.

HENRIETTA C. MEARS

∞

Prayer is simply intelligent, purposeful, devoted contact with God. Where that contact is established and maintained, prayer will work infallibly according to its own inherent laws.

CHARLES H. BRENT

∞

Prayer is the language of a man burdened with a sense of need. It is the voice of the beggar, conscious of his poverty, asking of another the things he needs. Not to pray is not only to declare there is nothing needed, but to admit to a non-realization of that need.

E. M. BOUNDS

∞

Prayer is a cry of hope.

FRENCH PROVERB

∞

Prayer at its highest is a two-way conversation —and to me the most important part is listening to God's replies.

FRANK C. LAUBACH

prayer is . . . .

1

Prayer is not monologue but dialogue; God's voice in response to mine is its most essential part. Listening to God's voice is the secret of the assurance that He will listen to mine.

ANDREW MURRAY

∞

Prayer is and remains always a native and deepest impulse of the soul of man…. Prayer is a turning of one's soul, in heroic reverence, in infinite desire and endeavor, towards the Highest, the All-Excellent, Omnipotent, Supreme.

THOMAS CARLYLE

∞

Prayer is the answer to every problem there is.

OSWALD CHAMBERS

Prayer is the contemplation of the facts of life from the highest point of view.

RALPH WALDO EMERSON

∞

Prayer is the most powerful form of energy one can generate. The influence of prayer on the human mind and body is as demonstrable as that of the secreting glands. Prayer is a force as real as terrestrial gravity. It supplies us with a flow of sustaining power in our daily lives.

ALEXIS CARREL

∞

Prayer is the spiritual gymnasium in which we exercise and practice Godliness.

V. L. CRAWFORD

prayer is . . .

1 Prayer is more than verbally filling in some requisition blank. It's fellowship with God! It's communion with the Lord through praising Him, rehearsing His promises, and then sharing our needs.

BILLY GRAHAM

∞

Prayer is the vital breath of the Christian; not the thing that makes him alive, but the evidence that he is alive.

OSWALD CHAMBERS

∞

Prayer is the soul getting into contact with the God in whom it believes.

HARRY EMERSON FOSDICK

Prayer is God's triumph of spiritual engineering, implying all His gifts and providing access to all the resources of His being. Prayer is a summit meeting in the very throne room of the universe. There is no higher level.

RALPH HERRING

∞

Prayer is the wing wherewith the soul flies to heaven; and meditation the eye with which we see God.

SAINT AMBROSE

∞

Prayer is not overcoming God's reluctance; it is laying hold of God's willingness.

GEORGIA HARKNESS

prayer is . . .

1

Prayer is the frame of the bridge from weeping to doing, built across the canyon of despair.

JAMES GILLIOM

∞

Prayer is a powerful thing, for God has bound and tied himself thereto. None can believe how powerful prayer is, and what it is able to effect, but those who have learned it by experience.

MARTIN LUTHER

∞

Prayer is the key that unlocks all the storehouses of God's infinite grace and power. All that God is and all that God has is at the disposal of prayer.

R. A. TORREY

Prayer is the soul's breathing itself into the bosom of its Heavenly Father.

THOMAS WATSON

∞

Prayer is intended to increase the devotion of the individual, but if the individual himself prays he requires no formulae.... Real inward devotion knows no prayer but that arising from the depths of its own feelings.

W. VON HUMBOLDT

∞

Prayer is a serious thing. We may be taken at our words.

DWIGHT L. MOODY

prayer is . . .

1

Prayer is a golden key which opens the morning and locks up the evening.

∞

Real prayer is taking His Word into the Throne Room and letting His words speak through your lips to Him on the throne, calling His attention to His own promises.

∞

Prayer is as vast as God because He is behind it. Prayer is as mighty as God because He has committed Himself to answer it.

Prayer is the gymnasium of the soul.

SAMUEL M. ZWEMER

∞

Prayer is conversation with God.

SAINT CLEMENT OF ALEXANDRIA

∞

Prayer is not eloquence but earnestness.

HANNAH MORE

∞

Prayer is the Christian's vital breath, the Christian's native air.

JAMES MONTGOMERY

prayer is . . .

1

Prayer is not only "the practice of the presence of God," it is the realization of His presence.

JOSEPH FORT NEWTON

∞

Prayer is a shield to the soul, a sacrifice to God, and a scourge to Satan.

JOHN BUNYAN

∞

Prayer is the cable, at whose end appears
The anchor hope, ne'er slipped but in our fears.

FRANCIS QUARLES

Prayer is the breath of the new-born soul, and there can be no Christian life without it.

ROWLAND HILL

∞

Prayer is releasing the energies of God. For prayer is asking God to do what we cannot do.

CHARLES TRUMBULL

∞

Prayer is not overcoming God's reluctance; it is laying hold of His highest willingness.

ARCHBISHOP RICHARD CHENEVIX
TRENCH

prayer is . . . .

1 Prayer is...talking with God and telling Him you love Him...conversing with God about all the things that are important in life, both large and small, and being assured that He is listening.

C. NEIL STRAIT

chapter two
intercession

"The Spirit helps us in our weakness. We
do not know what we ought to pray for,
but the Spirit himself intercedes for us."

ROMANS 8:26

∞

"I urge, then, first of all, that requests,
prayers, intercession and thanksgiving be
made for everyone."

1 TIMOTHY 2:1

Intercession is the mother tongue of the whole family of Christ.

DORA GREENWELL

intercession

The Mother Tongue

When we engage in intercession, we're acting on behalf of someone in difficulty, attempting to reconcile differences between people, pleading on someone else's behalf, or serving as a mediator. When we pray for others, we are intercessors between them and God, going to the Lord Himself on their behalf.

The cross on Calvary, where Jesus took on Himself the punishment for our sins, is the greatest example of intercession in the history of the world. In His own words: "For God did not send his Son into the world to condemn the world, but to save the world through him" (John 3:17).

Divine intercession on our behalf, however, did not end at the Cross. In Romans 8:26, the apostle Paul reminds us that even though we don't know what or how to pray, *"the [Holy] Spirit himself intercedes for us."* And in verse 34, he reports that Jesus Himself *"is at the right hand of God and is also interceding for us."*

Missionaries, pastors, Sunday-school teachers, and others in ministry are clearly engaged in intercession. The Great Commission states: *"Therefore go and make disciples of all nations, baptizing them in the name of the Father and of the Son and of the Holy Spirit"* (Matthew 28:19), and it is a command to us to intercede.

Intercession will not only have great impact on those for whom we intercede in prayer, but on ourselves as well. Consider the life of Job. Despite the incredible trials he endured—loss of family, possessions, and health—he remained faithful to God. Yet, as we read in Job 42:10, it wasn't until after Job interceded in prayer for his friends that his fortunes were restored.

In his book, The Meaning of Prayer, written in 1915, Harry Emerson Fosdick wrote: "Such prayer [intercession] does liberate. It carries a man out of himself; it brings to mind the names and needs of many friends, making the heart ready for service and the imagination apt to perceive ways of helping those else forgotten and neglected; it purges a man's spirit of vindictive moods and awakens every gracious and fraternal impulse."

Matthew Henry noted that "Christ intercedes for us in heaven, the Spirit intercedes for us in our hearts." Because Jesus is constantly interceding for us, should we not follow His example and pray for those around us? In doing so, we not only imitate Christ, but we invoke His power, the

2

power that can raise men from the dead, a power that can heal the sick, a power that can change lives and draw even the most hardhearted to Himself.

Is intercession an effective tool in today's world? An item in the November 19, 1999, edition of Federalist Brief *from* Publius Press *summarized a report in* The Archives of Internal Medicine *of a recent study conducted on 990 cardiac patients in St. Luke's Hospital in Kansas City, Missouri. As a research project, the patients were divided into two groups, and intercessors prayed for the individuals in one of them, knowing only their first names. "Neither the patients nor the medical staff knew the research was being conducted. Patients being prayed for did 11 percent better than those receiving usual care only."*

The editor of this medical journal commented: "This is a well-designed study.... If this was a medication, the conclusion would be that this medication helped." Even in today's jaded society, where prayer is banned in many places, it's clear that intercessory prayer is good medicine—that intercessory prayer is tremendous!

intercession

"Therefore

[Jesus Christ] is

able to save

completely those

who come to

God through

him, because

he always lives

to intercede

for them."

HEBREWS 7:25

Intercession leaves you neither time nor inclination to pray for your own "sad sweet self." The thought of yourself is not kept out because it is not there to keep out, you are completely and entirely identified with God's interest in other lives.

OSWALD CHAMBERS

"Pray for each other so that you may be healed. The prayer of a righteous man is powerful and effective."

JAMES 5:16

2

Do not let us fail one another in interest, care and practical help, but supremely we must not fail one another in prayer.

MICHAEL BAUGHEN

∞

Men may spurn our appeals, reject our message, oppose our arguments, despise our persons, but they are helpless against our prayers.

J. SIDLOW BAXTER

∞

Honest interceding is one of the means by which we come to a better understanding of God's will. Interceding causes us to look beyond our own needs to what God desires for mankind.

BOBB BIEHL/JAMES W. HAGELGANZ

Talking to men for God is a great thing, but talking to God for men is greater still.

E. M. BOUNDS

∞

By intercessory prayer we can hold off Satan from other lives and give the Holy Ghost a chance with them. No wonder Jesus put such tremendous emphasis on prayer!

OSWALD CHAMBERS

∞

The prayer of intercession is the...level of prayer in which we share the burden of Christ for a person, circumstance or need anywhere in the world.

PAUL Y. CHO

intercession

∞

2

Intercession…is love on its knees.

HARRY EMERSON FOSDICK

∞

Prayer is love raised to its greatest power; and the prayer of intercession is the noblest and most Christian kind of prayer because in it love—and imagination—reach their highest and widest range.

ROBERT J. MCCRACKEN

∞

Lord, help me live from day to day
In such a self-forgetful way,
That even when I kneel to pray,
My prayer shall be for—*others*.

CHARLES D. MEIGS

∞

In praying for people one dislikes I find it helpful to remember that one is joining in *His* prayer for them.

C. S. LEWIS

∞

When we pray for loved ones outside of Christ, we should expect them to come to Christ.

WILLIAM MCBIRNIE

∞

Many of us cannot reach the mission fields on our feet, but we can reach them on our knees. Solid lasting missionary work is accomplished by prayer, whether offered in China, India, or the United States.

J. O. FRASER

intercession

2 There are three things to be seen in an intercessor which are not necessarily found in ordinary prayer: identification, agony and authority.... Intercession so identifies the intercessor with the sufferer that it gives him a prevailing place with God.

NORMAN P. GRUBB

∽

He who prays for his neighbor will be heard for himself.

HEBREW PROVERB

∽

Those who always pray are necessary to those who never pray.

VICTOR HUGO

He that has once learned to know the Father in prayer for himself, learns to pray most confidently for others, too. The Father gives the Holy Spirit to them that ask Him, not least, but most, when they ask for others.

ANDREW MURRAY

∞

Distance is no bar, space no barrier, to reaching the remotest place on earth. Nor is the power of prayer diminished by the distance between the person who prays and the person who is prayed for. Men and nations can and do have their destinies decided by God's praying people who, through intercessory prayer, wield power greater than the armed might of the nations of the earth.

HAROLD LINDSELL

intercession

2

Intercession is the best arbitrator of all differences, the best promoter of true friendship, the best cure and preservative against all unkind tempers, all angry and haughty passions.

WILLIAM LAW

∞

Don't put people down—unless it's on your prayer list.

STAN MICHALSKI

∞

If I could hear Christ praying for me in the next room, I would not fear a million enemies. Yet distance makes no difference. He is praying for me.

ROBERT MURRAY MCCHEYNE

The prayer that we find hardest to comprehend, namely the intercessory, Jesus took most easily and naturally for granted.

FRANCIS J. MCCONNELL

∞

Nothing can so quickly cancel the frictions of life as prayers. "Praying hearts," it has been wisely said, "are forgiving hearts." So if we find ourselves growing angry at someone, pray for him—anger cannot live in the atmosphere of prayer.

WILLIAM T. MCELROY

∞

He causes his prayers to be of more avail to himself, who offers them also for others.

POPE GREGORY I

2

Can the humble request of believing lips restrain, accelerate, change the settled order of events? Can prayer make things that are not to be as though they were? Yes, a thousand times yes! Intercession is the mother tongue of the whole family of Christ.

DORA GREENWELL

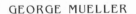

The great point is never to give up until the answer comes. I have been praying for 63 years and 8 months for one man's conversion. He is not saved yet, but he will be. How can it be otherwise? I am praying.

GEORGE MUELLER

There are particular things about which we ought to pray, for which we are commanded to pray; for all the saints, for the Word of God, for the Christian ministry, for all souls.

G. CAMPBELL MORGAN

∞

There is nothing that makes us love a man as much as praying for him.

WILLIAM LAW

∞

Intercession is simply love at prayer.

HENRIETTA C. MEARS

intercession

2

More things are wrought by prayer
Than this world dreams of. Wherefore,
    let thy voice
Rise like a fountain for me night and
    day.
For what are men better than sheep or
    goats
That nourish a blind life within the
    brain,
If, knowing God, they lift not hands of
    prayer
Both for themselves and those who call
    them friend?

ALFRED LORD TENNYSON

chapter three
answered prayer

"If you believe, you will receive whatever
you ask for in prayer."

MATTHEW 21:22

∞

"I will do whatever you ask in my name,
so that the Son may bring glory to the
Father. You may ask me for anything in
my name, and I will do it."

JOHN 14:13-14

When we pray for rain we should get
our umbrellas ready!

WILLIAM MCBIRNIE

answered prayer

Get Out Your Umbrella!

For many years, Dr. Dick Eastman, international president of Every Home for Christ in Colorado Springs, Colorado, has been a leading authority on prayer. He has served as president of the National Prayer Committee, has written several books and hundreds of articles on prayer, and has led countless thousands to a greater understanding of prayer through the Change the World School of Prayer, which he originated and leads all over the world.

3

In his School of Prayer manual, there's a story of answered prayer that is so powerful, so compelling that it has remained with us since we first heard it more than twenty years ago. The story itself took place back in the sixteenth century and involved one of Christianity's heroes, Martin Luther.

It seems that, in 1540, Luther's close friend and associate, Frederick Myconius, was near death and wrote a farewell letter to Luther. Luther's response: "I command thee in the name of God to live because I still have need of thee in the work of reforming the church…. The Lord will never let me hear that thou art dead, but will permit thee to survive me. For this I am praying, this is my will, and may my will be done, because I seek only to glorify the Name of God."

By then, Myconius's health had deteriorated to the point that death was imminent. Shortly after receiving Luther's letter, however, his condition began to change, and he eventually recovered *completely. Six years later, when Luther died, Myconius was still alive! Luther's prayer that his friend outlive him had been answered. Prayer, bold prayer, believing prayer, is tremendous!*

During the Civil War, the following item was discovered on the body of a fallen Confederate soldier. Although his identity was unknown, one thing was clear: He recognized how wonderfully God had answered his prayers, even though those answers had not been the ones he sought.

Answered Prayer

I asked God for strength, that I might
  achieve;
I was made weak, that I might learn
  humbly to obey.
I asked for health, that I might do
  greater things,
I was given infirmity that I might do
  better things.

answered prayer

3

I asked for riches, that I might be happy,
I was given poverty, that I might be
    wise.
I asked for power, that I might have the
    praise of men,
I was given weakness, that I might feel
    the need of God.
I asked for all things, that I might enjoy
    life,
I was given life, that I might enjoy all
    things.
I got nothing I asked for—but every-
    thing I had hoped for.
Almost despite myself my unspoken
    prayers were answered.
I am among all men most richly blessed.

*When we ask God for something and don't get
it, it's tempting to say, "God didn't answer my
prayer." So we become disillusioned and turn our*

backs on Him. It's important to recognize, however, as that soldier did, that there's a definite distinction between getting an answer to prayer and getting the answer we want and expect. Sometimes God's answer is "No," because He and He alone knows what's best for us, and often what we ask for is not. At other times, he may answer "Not now," because His timing, unlike ours, is always perfect.

As we ponder the following selections, let's keep in mind that God is not a genie in a bottle or some doting relative who'll give us whatever our little hearts desire. He's a kind, gentle, and wise heavenly Father who knows full well what's best for us.

"Call to me and I will answer you and tell you great and unsearchable things you do not know."

JEREMIAH 33:3

We do not receive things by prayer. We receive them by Jesus.

ARMIN GESSWEIN

"In my distress I called to the LORD,
and he answered me."
JONAH 2:2

3

I am not so sure that I believe in "the power of prayer," but I do believe in the power of the Lord who answers prayer.

DONALD GREY BARNHOUSE

∞

The whole canon of Bible teaching is to illustrate the great truth that God hears and answers prayer.

E. M. BOUNDS

∞

Some prayers have a longer voyage than others, but they return with the richer lading at last, so that the praying soul is a gainer by waiting for an answer.

WILLIAM GURNALL

God always answers us in the deeps, never in the shallows of our soul.

∞

God is not some cosmic bellboy for whom we can press a button to get things done.

∞

I know not by what methods rare,
But this I know: God answers prayer.
I know not if the blessings sought
Will come in just the guise I sought.
I leave my prayer to Him alone
Whose will is wiser than my own.

answered prayer

3

God's way of answering the Christian's prayer for more patience, experience, hope and love often is to put him into the furnace of affliction.

RICHARD CECIL

∞

I believe we get an answer to our prayers when we are willing to obey what is implicit in the answer. I believe that we get a vision of God when we are willing to accept what that vision does to us.

ELSIE CHAMBERLAIN

∞

Keep praying, but be thankful that God's answers are wiser than your prayers.

WILLIAM CULBERTSON

Though I am weak, yet God, when prayed,
Cannot withhold his conquering aid.

RALPH WALDO EMERSON

∞

If God is going to do it, it has to be by prayer.

ARMIN GESSWEIN

∞

It is by prayer that we couple the powers of
Heaven to our helplessness, the powers which
can turn water into wine and remove moun-
tains...the powers which can awaken those
who sleep in sin and raise up the dead, the
powers which can capture strongholds and
make the impossible possible.

O. HALLESBY

answered prayer

3 When we pray for rain we should get our umbrellas ready! When we pray for God's power, we should get ready to act.

WILLIAM MCBIRNIE

∞

The privilege of prayer, to me, is one of the most cherished possessions, because faith and experience alike convince me that God Himself sees and answers, and His answers I will never venture to criticize. It is only my part to ask.

WILFRED T. GRENFELL

∞

Prayer always has an effect even if it is not the effect we desire.

ALEXIS CARREL

We carry checks on the bank of heaven and never cash them at the window of prayer.... We lie to God in prayer if we do not rely on God after prayer.

VANCE HAVNER

∞

There are four ways God answers prayer: (1) No, not yet; (2) No, I love you too much; (3) Yes, I thought you'd never ask; (4) Yes, and here's more.

ANNE LEWIS

∞

Who rises from prayer a better man, his prayer is answered.

GEORGE MEREDITH

answered prayer

3

If you will pray in union to Jesus, having child-like confidence toward God...seeking the glory of God more than all personal benefits, I believe that in all such cases you will get the very thing you ask, at the very time you ask it.

ROBERT MURRAY MCCHEYNE

∞

I have lived to thank God that all my prayers have not been answered.

JEAN INGELOW

∞

I don't know of a single foreign product that enters this country untaxed except the answer to prayer.

MARK TWAIN

∞

Some people think that prayer just means asking for things, and if they fail to receive exactly what they asked for, they think the whole thing is a fraud.

GERALD VANN

∞

Many a fellow is praying for rain with his tub the wrong side up.

SAM JONES

∞

Do not mock God in your prayers. Do not beg Him to come to you. You know that He is never far from any soul that seeks Him. That prayer is answered before you utter it.

WALTER RAUSCHENBUSCH

∞ *answered prayer*

3

It would be well to remember the more we pray, the more power we have in prayer. Faith is not like gasoline, in danger of running out if we go too far. It is more like a muscle which strengthens from practice.

REX HUMBARD

∞

God does not hear us because of the length of our prayer, but because of the sincerity of it. Prayer is not to be measured by the yard, nor weighed by the pound. It is the might and force of it—the truth and reality of it—the energy and the intensity of it.

CHARLES H. SPURGEON

chapter four
learning to pray

4

"One day Jesus was praying in a certain place. When he finished, one of his disciples said to him, 'Lord, teach us to pray, just as John taught his disciples.'"

LUKE 11:1

He who has learned to pray has learned
the greatest secret of a holy and happy life.

WILLIAM LAW

learning to pray

The Greatest Secret

Why do we make prayer so complex? Do we spend so much time trying to learn what prayer is that we never actually get around to praying? "How to pray" has been the subject of many books, sermons, workshops, and seminars that have certainly helped thousands learn how to have more effective prayer lives.

Nevertheless, we believe that the very best way to learn how to pray is to follow the example of the disciples and seek the Lord

4

Himself as our teacher. Andrew Murray, the great nineteenth-century Scottish pastor, author, and prayer warrior, once wrote a brief study entitled "Lord, Teach Us to Pray." In it he says, "Though in its beginnings prayer is so simple that the feeblest child can pray, yet it is the highest and holiest work to which man can rise. It is fellowship with the Unseen and Most Holy One. The power of the eternal world has been placed at its disposal. Prayer is the very essence of true religion, the channel of all blessings, and the secret of power and life."

Murray cites many biblical examples of God's people seeking Him in prayer and of the wonders their prayers accomplished. Certainly, no book ever written on prayer can begin to compare with the Bible, the very Word of God. Every aspect of prayer, Murray writes, "is revealed through His Word. Amid the painful consciousness of igno-

rance and unworthiness, we learn the heavenly art of effective prayer.

"When the deep undertone of all our prayer is the teachableness that comes from a sense of our ignorance, and from faith in Him as a perfect Teacher, we may be sure we shall be taught; we shall learn to pray in power. Yes, we may depend upon it: He teaches us to pray."

Murray then examines each phrase the Lord used in answering the disciples' request to teach them to pray. Indeed, The Lord's Prayer contains everything we need to know in order to learn how to pray. In it, we find adoration, intercession, submission, petition, confession, and pleas for forgiveness and deliverance.

There's another very important aspect of prayer that Jesus taught His followers: During their last meal together before His crucifixion, He repeatedly instructed them to ask "in my name"

4 (John 14:13–14; 15:16; 16:23–24, 26). It is, in effect, a divine "power of attorney," authorizing us to draw upon the infinite resources of our heavenly Father in the name of His beloved Son, the Lord Jesus Christ.

Certainly it's important to learn as much as we can about perhaps the most important topic in the world, but what we really need to do is pray.

Prayer has been called "a dialogue with a loved one," a "conversation with God." We carry on conversations every day, without spending too much time studying them. As many of the following comments remind us, we learn to pray by praying.

The little girl in the following story hadn't learned how to pray, but she just went ahead and prayed anyway, trusting God to put it all together. May we do the same.

A Child's Prayer

A man passed his granddaughter's room one night and overheard her repeating the alphabet in an oddly reverent way. He asked her, "What on earth are you up to?" She explained, "I'm saying my prayers, but I can't think of exactly the right words tonight, so I'm just saying all the letters. God will put them together for me, because He knows what I'm thinking."

AUTHOR UNKNOWN

learning to pray

Praying is the best school
in which to learn to pray,
prayer the best dictionary
to define the art and the
nature of praying.

E. M. BOUNDS

IN our praying we draw on our memories, on our past experiences, on our present desires. We only learn to draw on the grace of God by pureness, by knowledge, by long-suffering.

OSWALD CHAMBERS

4

Don't get the idea that if you can only muster up faith, you will be effective in prayer. Faith is not some mysterious commodity to be sought after. You do not need more faith; you need to learn how to appropriate the faith you already have.

JOHN BISAGNO

∞

No man ever prayed heartily without learning something.

RALPH WALDO EMERSON

∞

For a successful season of prayer, the best beginning is confession.

CHARLES H. SPURGEON

The main lesson about prayer is just this: *Do it! Do it! Do it!* You want to be *taught* to pray? My answer is: pray.

JOHN LAIDLAW

∞

To pray strenuously needs careful cultivation. We have to learn the most natural methods of expressing ourselves to our Father.

OSWALD CHAMBERS

∞

We can read all the books that have ever been written about prayer, but until we actually choose by an act of our will, to pray, we will never learn.

HOPE MACDONALD

learning to pray

4

I'd rather be able to pray than be a great preacher; Jesus Christ never taught his disciples how to preach, but only how to pray.

DWIGHT L. MOODY

∞

When the Spirit prays through us, he trims our praying down to the will of God.... The Holy Spirit is both teacher and lesson. We pray, not by the truth he reveals to us, but we pray by the actual presence of the Holy Spirit. He kindles the desire in hearts by his own flame.

E. M. BOUNDS

∞

Books on prayer are good, but not good enough. As books on cooking are good but hopeless unless there is food to work on, so with prayer.

One can read a library of prayer books and not be one whit more powerful in prayer. We must learn to pray, and we must pray to learn to pray.

LEONARD RAVENHILL

∞

Prayer is putting the lens of your soul on time exposure. Prayer is putting on earphones that shut out all noises but the voice of you and your God. Prayer always has, along with its receptivity, four statements: "Thank You. I'm sorry. Teach me. God with me."

JAMES GILLIOM

∞

Perhaps the greatest single difficulty in maintaining the habit of prayer is our tendency to make of it a *pious form* and not a *vital transaction*.

learning to pray

4

We begin by trying to pray and end up saying prayers...but if the act of prayer can be seen as...a vital and sustaining friendship with a God who cares for every one of us, praying will cease being a form and become a force and a privilege.

HARRY EMERSON FOSDICK

Our Lord's teaching about prayer is so amazingly simple but at the same time so amazingly profound that we are apt to miss His meaning. The danger is to water down what Jesus says about prayer and make it mean something more common sense; if it were common sense, it was not worth His while to say it. The things Jesus says about prayer are supernatural revelations.

OSWALD CHAMBERS

In the long run it is only prayer that can teach us what to pray for. Sooner or later we make Charlotte Bronte's prayer our own: "Grant us, O Lord, so to pray as to deserve to be heard." And then we learn that some prayers do not even deserve to be said.

ROGER HAZELTON

∞

The closet where we speak to God is not very well lit—but the light that filters into it has a quality of its own; it is a ray of the Eternal Light on which we cannot easily look; but as we get used to it, sun ourselves in its glow, we learn, as we can bear it, to see more and more.

EVELYN UNDERHILL

learning to pray

4

To pray is nothing more involved than to let Jesus into our needs. To pray is to give Jesus permission to apply His power in the alleviation of our distress. To pray is to let Jesus glorify His name in the midst of our needs. To pray is nothing more involved than to open the door, giving Jesus access to our needs and permitting Him to exercise His own power in dealing with them.

O. HALLESBY

∞

We can read all the books that have ever been written about prayer, but until we actually choose by an act of our will, to pray, we will never learn.

HOPE MACDONALD

∞

The law of prayer is the law of harvest: sow sparingly in prayer, reap sparingly; sow bountifully in prayer, reap bountifully. The trouble is that we are trying to get from our efforts what we never put into them.

LEONARD RAVENHILL

∞

If we are willing to take hours on end to learn to play a piano, or operate a computer, or fly an airplane, it is sheer nonsense for us to imagine that we can learn the high art of getting guidance through communion with the Lord without being willing to set aside time for it. It is no accident that the Bible speaks of prayer as a form of waiting on God.

PAUL S. REES

learning to pray

4

In our Lord's teaching about petitionary prayer there are three main principles. The first is confidence, the second is perseverance, and the third, for lack of a better word, I will call correspondence with Christ.

WILLIAM TEMPLE

∞

I would have no other desire than to accomplish thy will. Teach me to pray; pray thyself in me.

FRANCOIS FENELON

∞

Be honest in your secret prayer. Do not express any want that you do not feel. Do not confess

92

any fault that you do not mean to forsake. Do not keep anything back. Remember that it is He that searcheth the heart to whom you are speaking.

WALTER RAUSCHENBUSCH

∞

In listening prayer, we must learn to quiet our bodies and our minds and put ourselves in a receptive attitude, an attitude of waiting, of listening.

JO KIMMEL

∞

Faith is the bucket of power lowered by the rope of prayer into the well of God's abundance. What we bring up depends upon what

learning to pray

4 we let down. We have every encouragement
to use a big bucket.

VIRGINIA WHITMAN

∞

If I am right, Thy grace impart,
Still in the right to stay;
If I am wrong, O teach my heart
To find that better way!

ALEXANDER POPE

∞

O Thou by whom we come to God
The Life, the Truth, the Way—
The path of prayer Thyself hath trod,
Lord, teach us how to pray.

AUTHOR UNKNOWN

praise and thanksgiving

5

"It is good to praise the LORD and make
music to your name, O Most High."

PSALM 92:1

∞

"From the rising of the sun to the place
where it sets, the name of the LORD is
to be praised."

PSALM 113:3

Thou who hast given so much to me, give one
thing more—a grateful heart!

GEORGE HERBERT

five 5

praise and
thanksgiving

Grateful Hearts

It's so easy for us to be grateful when everything's going our way, but it becomes very difficult to maintain that attitude when the road gets rough, when a loved one dies, when we become ill, or when financial reverses strike. As the following prayer of George Matheson, nineteenth-century, blind Scottish preacher, reminds us, we need to have a thankful spirit even in times of trial, confident that God has promised to be with us always and to never leave us or forsake us.

5

"My God, I have never thanked Thee for my thorn. I have thanked Thee a thousand times for my roses, but not once for my thorn. I have been looking forward to a world where I shall get compensation for my cross; but I have never thought of my cross as itself a present glory. Teach me the glory of my cross; teach me the value of my thorn. Show me that I have climbed to Thee by the path of pain. Show me that my tears have made my rainbows."

Closely intertwined with an attitude of gratitude should be one of praise, praise to God because of who He is and because of all He has done for us. An excellent definition we once heard was in the form of an acrostic: "PRAISE—Publicly Recounting the Acts of the Incomparable Sovereign of Eternity."

Some might ask why it's important to praise God. Certainly He has no need of our praises.

Nor will all the praise in the world change Him in any way. Instead, praising God changes us.

Another word for "praise" that's often used in Scripture is "magnify." If we were to look at the words on this page through a magnifying glass, it would not change their size, shape, or meaning in any way. All that would change would be our perception, as the words would appear larger and clearer than before.

So it is when we praise or magnify God. He isn't changed, but our perception of Him is—we see Him in a new light, from a new perspective, and more clearly than before.

A powerful illustration of this principle was demonstrated in the life of a man named Morris M. Townsend, a distinguished New York financial consultant and government official. Shortly before his death in 1967, Townsend wrote a letter that included the following: "It has pleased God in His

5

sovereignty to put cancer in both of my lungs and in my liver, and it is the fast-spreading type.... *This has been a time of great rejoicing for my wife and me because His joy, His peace and His presence have just overshadowed everything else, and we would not change one minute of it if we could."*

Townsend closed his letter with some sound words of advice for all of us: "Rejoice with us in the reality of His presence twenty-four hours a day."

Dr. Bob Snyder, a former emergency-room physician here in the United States, left his practice to become a missionary in Hungary. Every week, he sends excerpts from his journal, Lessons Learned on the Journey, back home to friends and supporters. On a recent Thanksgiving Day, he wrote: "Does gratitude have any medical benefit? I can't prove any physical benefit scientifically. However it does have eternal benefit. Gratitude expressed in praise and thanksgiving is the attitude in which every follower of Jesus should live."

Praise and thanksgiving—tremendous twin keys to draw us ever closer to our God.

"Be joyful always;...
give thanks in all circumstances,
for this is God's will for you in
Christ Jesus."

1 THESSALONIANS 5:16, 18

"Enter his gates with thanksgiving and his courts with
praise; give thanks to him and
praise his name."

PSALM 100:4

It will be a foretaste of heaven to us here below, if we are able to thank God for all His infinite goodness with all our heart.

OTTOKAR PROHASZKA

5

Through all eternity to Thee
    A grateful song I'll raise;
But oh! Eternity's too short
    To utter all Thy praise.

JOSEPH ADDISON

∞

Praise is almost the only thing we do on earth that we shall not cease to do in heaven.

SAMUEL BRENGLE

∞

Praise is the best auxiliary to prayer. He who most bears in mind what has been done for him by God will be most emboldened to ask for fresh gifts from above.

ANDREW MELVILLE

Prayer crowns God with the honor and glory
due to His name.

THOMAS BENTON BROOKS

∞

Too often we forget to thank God for
answered prayer. Praise is the proper punctua-
tion mark for an answered prayer.

CADLE CALL

∞

Our Father in heaven…if we do not have the
grace to thank Thee for all that we have and
enjoy, how can we have the effrontery to seek
Thy further blessings? God, give us grateful
hearts. For Jesus' sake. Amen.

PETER MARSHALL

praise and thanksgiving

5

One of the most essential preparations for eternity is delight in praising God; a higher requirement, I do think, than even delight and devotedness in prayer.

THOMAS CHALMERS

Gratitude does nothing but love God because of the greatness of His bounty and proclaims His goodness unceasingly.

OTTOKAR PROHASZKA

Lord, we're not just thankful for what You give us. We are thankful most of all for the privilege of learning to be thankful.

CHARLIE "TREMENDOUS" JONES

The worship most acceptable to God comes from a thankful and cheerful heart.

PLUTARCH

∞

The greatest saint in the world is not he who prays most or fasts most; it is not he who gives alms, or is most eminent for temperance, chastity or justice. It is he who is most thankful to God, and who has a heart always ready to praise Him.

WILLIAM LAW

∞

You don't have to be afraid of praising God too much; unlike humans He never gets a big head.

PAUL DIBBLE

5

It is always possible to be thankful for what is given rather than to complain about what is not given. One or the other becomes a habit of life.

ELISABETH ELLIOT

∞

Praise is like a plow set to go deep into the soil of believers' hearts. It lets the glory of God into the details of daily living.

C. M. HANSON

∞

The continual offering of praise requires stamina; we ought to praise God even when we do not feel like it. Praising him takes away the blues and restores us to normal.

HAROLD LINDSELL

∞

Thanksgiving is nothing if not a glad and reverent lifting of the heart to God in honour and praise for His goodness.

JAMES R. MILLER

∞

Thou who hast given so much to me,
Give one thing more—a grateful heart;
Not thankful when it pleaseth me,
As if Thy blessings had spare days;
But such a heart, whose pulse may be
    Thy praise.

GEORGE HERBERT

∞

No prayer is complete without praise.

ANONYMOUS

5

Praise God even when you don't understand what He is doing.

HENRY JACOBSEN

∞

The very act of prayer honors God and gives glory to God, for it confesses that God is what He is.

CHARLES KINGSLEY

∞

It is probable that in most of us the spiritual life is impoverished and stunted because we give so little place to gratitude. It is more important to thank God for blessings received than to pray for them beforehand.

WILLIAM TEMPLE

For three things I thank God every day of my life: thanks that He has vouchsafed me knowledge of His Works; deep thanks that He has set in my darkness the lamp of faith; deep, deepest thanks that I have another life to look forward to—a life joyous with light and flowers and heavenly song.

HELEN KELLER

Fountain of mercy! Whose pervading eye
Can look within and read what passes there,
Accept my thoughts for thanks; I have
   no words.
My soul, o'erfraught with gratitude rejects
The aid of language—
Lord, behold my heart.

HANNAH MORE

5

No duty is more urgent than that of returning thanks.

SAINT AMBROSE

∞

The Christian should be an *alleluia* from head to foot.

SAINT AUGUSTINE

∞

O Lord, that lends me life, lend me a heart replete with thankfulness.

WILLIAM SHAKESPEARE

∞

The unmistakable mark of a living faith is a readiness to praise.

HOWARD H. JONES

∞

God gave you the gift of 86,400 seconds today. Have you used one to say "thank you"?

WILLIAM A. WARD

∞

All that I see teaches me to thank the Creator for all I cannot see.

HENRIETTA C. MEARS

5

Now thank we all our God
　　　With heart and hands and voices
Who wondrous things hath done,
　　　In whom His world rejoices.

MARTIN RINKART

∞

I have never committed the least matter to God that I have not had reason for infinite praise.

ANNA SHIPTON

∞

The worst moment for the atheist is when he is really thankful, and has nobody to thank.

DANTE GABRIEL ROSETTI

chapter six
when to pray

"*Jesus went out to a mountainside to pray, and spent the night praying to God.*"

LUKE 6:12

∞

"*Then Jesus told his disciples a parable to show them that they should always pray and not give up.*"

LUKE 18:1

We can come anytime, in any place, with
our bodies in any position.

WARREN MYERS

six

6

when to pray

Any Time, Any Place

Several hundred years ago, a humble monk named Brother Lawrence wrote a series of letters about his intimate relationship with God, a relationship that was part of every moment of his day. These letters, along with a record of some of his conversations, were later published in a small book entitled The Practice of the Presence of God, *which has become a classic of Christian literature.*

In it, Brother Lawrence, a Frenchman whose real name was Nicholas Herman, is quoted as saying, "The time of business

6

does not with me differ from the time of prayer, and in the noise and clatter of my kitchen, while several persons are at the same time calling for different things, I possess God in as great tranquility as if I were upon my knees at that blessed sacrament."

It made no difference to Brother Lawrence where he was or what he was doing. In the kitchen or on his knees, he kept the Lord with him constantly. In our hectic lives, we can do the same. Prayer isn't some formal exercise to be practiced only in church, at mealtime, or beside our beds at night. We can, and should, pray throughout the day: when we're driving our cars (with eyes open, please), at work or play, at mealtimes, and throughout every waking hour.

In this high-tech, fast-everything world of ours, we hear a lot about 24/7. Standing for twenty-four hours a day, seven days a week, it's become a kind of shorthand for round-the-clock availability. For example, e-commerce—transacting business or shopping for virtually anything via computer—promises and delivers 24/7 service, without your ever having to leave home.

A new concept? Hardly! From all eternity, God has been available—24/7! We once heard a preacher refer to Jeremiah 33:3 ("Call to me and I will answer you...") as "God's telephone number." It doesn't say "between the hours of nine and five" or "at bedtime," and you never get a busy signal or voice mail.

An eight-year-old boy named Danny Dutton understood the divine 24/7 concept. In an essay entitled "Explaining God," he pointed out that one of God's "most important jobs is listening to prayers." He adds, "An awful lot of this goes on, as some people, like preachers and things, pray other times besides bedtime. God doesn't have

6

time to listen to the radio or TV on account of this."

We, too, can "pray other times besides bedtime," knowing that God always hears our prayers. The following quotes help remind us that prayer is appropriate at any time. Now, that's tremendous!

Most of us have much trouble praying when we are in little trouble, but we have little trouble praying when we are in much trouble.

RICHARD P. COOK

"*Pray continually.*"
1 THESSALONIANS 5:17

Lift up your heart to Him, sometimes even at your meals, and when you are in company; the least little remembrance will always be acceptable to Him.

BROTHER LAWRENCE

6

Let our prayers, like the ancient sacrifices, ascend morning and evening. Let our days begin and end with God.

WILLIAM ELLERY CHANNING

∞

Pray your way through the day. You can't see around the turning of life's corners, but God can. When the alarm goes off, instead of saying, "Good Lord—morning!" say, "Good morning, Lord."

ROBERT A. COOK

∞

Prayer should be the key of the morning and the lock of the night.

OWEN FELLTHAM

Dear Lord, who sought at dawn of day,
In solitary woods to pray.
In quietness we come to ask
Thy presence for our daily task.

HARRY WEBB FARRINGTON

∞

We can come anytime, in any place, with our bodies in any position—kneeling, sitting, standing, walking, or even jogging.

WARREN MYERS

∞

If you do not feel like praying, it is probably a good indication that you should start praying immediately.

BILLY GRAHAM

6

It is well to let prayer be the first employment in the early morning and the last in the evening. Avoid diligently those false and deceptive thoughts which say, "I will pray an hour hence; I must first perform this or that." For with such thoughts a man quits prayer for business, which lays hold of and entangles him so that he comes not to pray the whole day long.

MARTIN LUTHER

I have so much to do that I must spend several hours in prayer before I am able to do it.

JOHN WESLEY

Our failure to think of prayer as a privilege may be partly due to the fact that we can pray any time. The door to prayer is open so continuously that we fail to avail ourselves of an opportunity that is always there.

HARRY EMERSON FOSDICK

∞

When everyone seemed panic-stricken...I went to my room...and got down on my knees before Almighty God and prayed.... Soon a great comfort crept into my soul that God Almighty had taken the whole business into His own hands.

ABRAHAM LINCOLN

when to pray

6

The Bible doesn't say we should preach all the time, but it does say we should pray all the time.

JOHN R. RICE

∞

Morning prayer: Good morning, God, I love You! What are you up to today? I want to be part of it.

NORMAN GRUBB

∞

Do not have your concert first, then tune your instrument afterwards. Begin the day with the Word of God and prayer, and get first of all in harmony with Him.

J. HUDSON TAYLOR

∞

It is good to pray for the repair of mistakes, but praying earlier would keep us from making so many.... When puzzled, go to prayer and listen.

J. C. MACAULAY

∞

The man who says his prayers in the evening is a captain posting his sentries. After that, he can sleep.

CHARLES BAUDELAIRE

∞

If you have ever prayed in the dawn you will ask yourself why you were so foolish as not to do it always: it is difficult to get into communion with God in the midst of the hurly-burly of the day.

OSWALD CHAMBERS

when to pray

129

6

In a single day I have prayed as many as a hundred times, and in the night almost as often.

SAINT PATRICK

∞

To be with God, there is no need to be continually in church. We may make an oratory of our heart wherein to retire from time to time to converse with Him in meekness, humility and love. There is not in the world a kind of life more sweet and delightful than that of a continual conversation with God.

BROTHER LAWRENCE

presenting your requests

"Hear the supplication of your servant [Solomon] and of your people Israel when they pray.... Hear from heaven, your dwelling place, and when you hear, forgive."

1 KINGS 8:30

The sweetest lesson I have learned in God's school is to let the Lord choose for me.

DWIGHT L. MOODY

seven 7

presenting your requests

The Sweetest Lesson

As we've already seen, there is far more to prayer than asking for things. Yet too often, the only time we pray is when we want or need something, and then we look on God as a sort of benevolent Santa Claus, whose job is to grant our every wish.

When we do bring our petitions before the Lord, the first thing we should ask for is forgiveness of our sins, a request He has promised He will always grant. In 1 John 1:9, we read: "If we confess our sins, he is faithful and just and will forgive us

7

our sins and purify us from all unrighteousness." Then we can stand clean and forgiven before Him.

Again, it's important to remember that prayer and petition are not synonymous. God is all-knowing and all-powerful, and He loves us with an everlasting love. Prayer is the primary means He has provided for us to get to know Him, to have communion with Him, to listen to Him, and to speak to Him.

God knows our every need and every desire of our hearts. When we bring our petitions before Him, we need to do so in a spirit of trust and of patience, recognizing that God's will for us is perfect and that His answers will always be given in the light of what's best for us. As the late Morris Townsend wrote, just before his death from cancer in 1967, "It would be incredible to think that our Father, who has built a hedge about us, even as he did about Job—yes, incredible—to think that He would send or let anything get through that hedge that was not good for us."

Jesus Himself set the example for us. Facing a horrible death, He prayed that His Father would spare Him, but He quickly added, "Not my will, but Thine be done." May this be our attitude when we bring our petitions to Him.

"*Delight* yourself in the Lᴏʀᴅ and he will give you the desires of your heart."

PSALM 37:4

"Do not be anxious about anything, but in everything, by prayer and petition, with thanksgiving, present your requests to God."

PHILIPPIANS 4:6

7 Before prayer ever starts toward God, before its petition is preferred, before its requests are made known—faith must have gone on ahead; must have asserted its belief in the existence of God; must have given its assent to the gracious truth that "God is a rewarder of those that diligently seek His face."

E. M. BOUNDS

∞

Is prayer your steering wheel or your spare tire?

CORRIE TEN BOOM

∞

The purpose of all prayer is to find God's will and to make that will our prayer.

CATHERINE MARSHALL

138

Prayers are heard in heaven very much in proportion to our faith. Little faith will get very great mercies, but great faith still greater.

CHARLES H. SPURGEON

∞

We should be as specific in our requests when in prayer to God as we are when we need a definite item at the market.

SAMUEL BRENGLE

∞

The first thing that should concern you in your conversation with God is personal cleansing. Before you pray for a change of circumstances, you should pray for a change in character.

JOHN LAVENDER

presenting your requests

7

Prayer is not a vain attempt to change God's will; it is a filial desire to learn God's will and to share it.

GEORGE A. BUTTRICK

∞

Lord, make me more like Yourself, less like myself.

LESTER CASE

∞

There cannot be any touching of the Master without the Master knowing it. When need touches Him, it makes a demand upon His ability to meet that need; and prayer is the way in which we touch Him.

E. W. KENYON

Prayer reminds us of our constant need for God and reassures us of His presence with us. Prayer is part of God's plan for our growth and for His program in the world. In prayer, we don't tell God what to do; we find out what He wants us to do.

DAVID HUBBARD

∞

The biggest problem in prayer is how to "let go and let God."

GLENN CLARK

∞

To pray is nothing more involved than to lie in the sunshine of God's grace.

O. HALLESBY

7

Really to pray is to stand to attention in the presence of the King and to be prepared to take orders from Him.

DONALD COGGAN

∞

To pray...is to desire; but it is to desire what God would have us desire. He who desires not from the bottom of his heart offers a deceitful prayer.

FRANCOIS FENELON

∞

There are two kinds of people: those who say to God, "Thy will be done," and those to whom God says, "All right, then, have it your way."

C. S. LEWIS

Spread out your petition before God, and then say, "Thy will, not mine, be done." The sweetest lesson I have learned in God's school is to let the Lord choose for me.

DWIGHT L. MOODY

∞

Prayer is not an easy way of getting what we want, but the only way of becoming what God wants us to be.

STUDDERT KENNEDY

∞

Ordinarily when a man in difficulty turns to prayer, he has already tried every other means of escape.

AUSTIN O'MALLEY

presenting your requests

7

How often we look upon God as our last resource! We go to him because we have nowhere else to go. And then we learn that the storms of life have driven us, not upon the rocks, but into the desired haven.

GEORGE MACDONALD

∞

I MUST remember that God is not my private secretary.

FLORENCE NIGHTINGALE

∞

What we usually pray to God is not that His will be done, but that He approve ours.

HELGA BERGOLD GROSS

∞

God insists that we ask, not because *He* needs to know our situation, but because *we* need the spiritual discipline of asking.

CATHERINE MARSHALL

∞

Prayer enlarges the heart until it is capable of containing God's gift of Himself.

MOTHER TERESA

∞

A God who filled the prayer-orders of people whose wills were not His own would be no God at all. He would be a heavenly vending machine.

MALCOLM NYGREN

presenting your requests

7 Don't bother to give God instructions; just report for duty.

CORRIE TEN BOOM

∞

Whether we like it or not, asking is the rule of the Kingdom.

CHARLES H. SPURGEON

chapter eight
counsel and observations

"*Call upon me in the day of trouble; I will deliver you.*"

PSALM 50:15

Let's keep our chins up and our knees down—
we're on the victory side!

ALAN REDPATH

counsel and observations

Chins Up, Knees Down

Many verses from Scripture represent wise counsel indeed, but they are far more than that; they are the sacred promises of God Himself. Down through the centuries, such men of faith as John Bunyan, author of that magnificent Christian classic Pilgrim's Progress, the great Saint Augustine, the humble Brother Lawrence, and other giants of the faith have claimed those promises and followed that divine counsel.

8

It was men of like mind who founded this great nation of ours on a bedrock of prayer, men who recognized their complete and absolute dependence on Almighty God. Virtually all our early presidents, beginning with George Washington, were strong believers in the power of prayer. Both publicly and privately, Washington frequently referred to his dependence on Almighty God.

In 1873, shortly after the successful conclusion of the Revolutionary War and six years before he would become our first president, Washington composed a Prayer for the United States of America. In it he acknowledged that without the guiding hand of God, "we can never hope to be a happy nation."

Washington's successor as president, John Adams, was also a firm believer in God, as evidenced by a prayer that has become a permanent reminder to those who have come after him.

Although plans for a permanent presidential home began during Washington's administration, Adams was the first to occupy the White House. In a letter to his wife, Abigail, written shortly after moving in, he said: "I pray Heaven to bestow the best of blessings on this house and all that shall hereafter inhabit it. May none but honest and wise men ever rule under this roof."

More than a century later, President Franklin D. Roosevelt had that prayer carved on the mantel of the State Dining Room.

How ironic that the leaders of a nation founded by such men no longer allow prayers to be posted in public places or included in public ceremonies. Could these men—who came to America because of a burning desire to be free to pray and worship the divine Creator of the universe—have ever imagined that in today's American society, students who pray aloud in public would be subjected

8

to government-ordained persecution for voicing their faith in Almighty God? It would have been incomprehensible to them!

How wise we would be to follow the example of another great American president, Abraham Lincoln, who said: "I have been driven many times upon my knees by the overwhelming conviction that I had nowhere else to go." How much wiser still to heed the words of God Himself: "If my people, who are called by my name, will humble themselves and pray and seek my face and turn from their wicked ways, then will I hear from heaven and will forgive their sin and will heal their land" (2 Chronicles 7:14).

The best time to stand
up to any of life's situations is
immediately after you get up
from praying on your knees.

O. A. BATTISTA

"Ask and it will be given to
you; seek and you will find;
knock and the door will be
opened to you."

MATTHEW 7:7

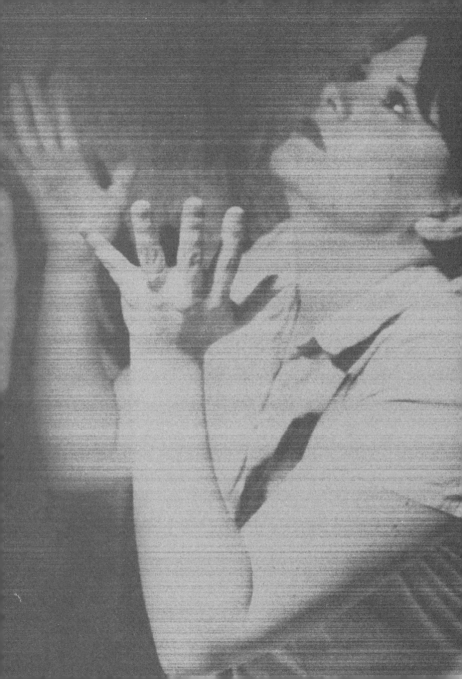

8

Labor at prayer, and then watch God work.

HENRIETTA C. MEARS

∞

Do not pray for easy lives. Pray to be stronger men! Do not pray for tasks equal to your powers. Pray for powers equal to your tasks. Then the doing of your work shall be no miracle, but you shall be a miracle.

PHILLIPS BROOKS

∞

Talk to him in prayer of all your wants, your troubles, even of the weariness you feel in serving him. You cannot speak too freely, too trustfully, to him.

FRANCOIS FENELON

Where God is concerned the only language open to us is prayer.

J. H. OLDHAM

∞

Those who pray for a million dollars would get better results if they prayed for a strong back and a good pair of hands.

O. A. BATTISTA

∞

Let all of us...give thanks to God and prayerful contemplation of those eternal truths and universal principles of Holy Scripture which have inspired such measure of true greatness as this nation has achieved.

DWIGHT D. EISENHOWER

8

America was founded by people who believed that God was their rock of safety. I recognize we must be cautious in claiming that God is on our side, but I think it's all right to keep asking if we're on His side.

RONALD REAGAN

∞

If you would have God hear you when you pray, you must hear Him when He speaks.

THOMAS BENTON BROOKS

∞

Our one great business is prayer, and we will never do it well unless we fasten to it by all binding force.

E. M. BOUNDS

If you are swept off your feet, it's a good time
to get on your knees.

FRED BECK

∞

We ought to act with God in the greatest sim-
plicity, speaking to Him frankly and plainly,
and imploring His assistance in our affairs, just
as they happen.

BROTHER LAWRENCE

∞

We should pray with as much earnestness as
those who expect everything from God; we
should act with as much energy as those who
expect everything from themselves.

CHARLES CALEB COLTON

8

The self-sufficient do not pray, the self-satisfied will not pray, the self-righteous cannot pray. No man is greater than his prayer life.

LEONARD RAVENHILL

In prayer it is better to have a heart without words than words without a heart.

JOHN BUNYAN

I nightly offer up my prayers to the throne of grace...that we ought all to rely with confidence on the promises of our dear Redeemer, and give Him our hearts.

ANDREW JACKSON

A prayer, in its simplest definition, is merely a wish turned heavenward.

PHILLIPS BROOKS

∞

We all can pray. We all should pray. We should ask the fulfillment of God's will. We should ask for courage, wisdom, for the quietness of soul which comes alone to them who place their lives in His hands.

HARRY S. TRUMAN

∞

Put your life into your prayer, and let it be the most real and most immediate business of your life.

WALTER RAUSCHENBUSCH

counsel and observations

161

8

If you can't pray a door open, don't pry it open.

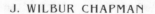

He prays well who is so absorbed with God that he does not know he is praying.

SAINT FRANCIS DE SALES

It is not...the Christian in the world but the world in the Christian that constitutes the danger. Anything that dims my vision of Christ, or takes away my taste for Bible study, or cramps my prayer life...is wrong for me.

J. WILBUR CHAPMAN

Pray as though everything depended on God.
Work as though everything depended on you.

SAINT AUGUSTINE

∞

Pray on! Pray on! Cease not to pray,
And should the answer tarry, WAIT!
Thy God will come, will surely come,
And He can never come too late.

AUTHOR UNKNOWN

∞

Those who pray for a million dollars would get
better results if they prayed for a strong back and
a good pair of hands.

O. A. BATTISTA

counsel and observations

8 God's ear is constantly to your lips. You cannot even breathe a prayer without His hearing it.

HENRIETTA C. MEARS

What the church needs today is not more machinery or better, nor new organizations or more and novel methods, but men whom the Holy Ghost can use—men of prayer, men mighty in prayer. The Holy Ghost does not flow through methods, but through men. He does not come on machinery, but on men. He does not anoint plans, but men—men of prayer.

E. M. BOUNDS